WHSmith

Challenge
English
KS2: Year 3
Age 7–8

Louis Fidge

Text and illustrations © Hodder Education

First published in 2007
exclusively for WHSmith by
Hodder Education
338 Euston Road
London NW1 3BH

Impression number   10 9 8 7 6 5 4 3 2 1
Year   2010 2009 2008 2007

Cover illustration by Sally Newton Illustrations

Typeset by Servis Filmsetting Ltd, Manchester

Printed and bound in UK by CPI Bath

A CIP record for this book is available from the
British Library

ISBN: 978 0 340 94546 9

Contents

Parents' notes

How this series can help your child

- The *WHS Challenge* series provides a wide range of activities that will stretch and challenge your child.
- It offers a straightforward, no-nonsense approach to basic English skills.
- It is carefully graded and provides a continuous development of essential English skills throughout Key Stage 2.
- There is comprehensive coverage of the skills that form part of the National Curriculum.
- Regular tests are included so progress and achievement can clearly be seen.
- The series gives your child confidence to face the different types of tests in school.
- It helps to improve your child's results in school.
- It is designed to be used alongside any English course your child is using.
- Its clear, accessible format offers rigour, support and structure.

Using this book

- There are 24 topics and 4 tests in the book. A test occurs after 6 topics have been completed.
- Each topic need not be completed in one session. Think of it as about a week's work.
- Do give help and encouragement. Completing the activities should not become a chore.
- Do let your child mark his or her own work under your supervision and correct any careless mistakes he or she might have made.
- When all the tests have been completed, let your child fill in the Certificate of Achievement on the opposite page.
- Each double page has a title, explanation of the learning point, practice section, and challenge section.

Topic – the main learning point

Get started – helpful information and tips about the learning point

Practice – straightforward follow-up to the learning point

Challenge – uses the learning point in a slightly different way and takes it further

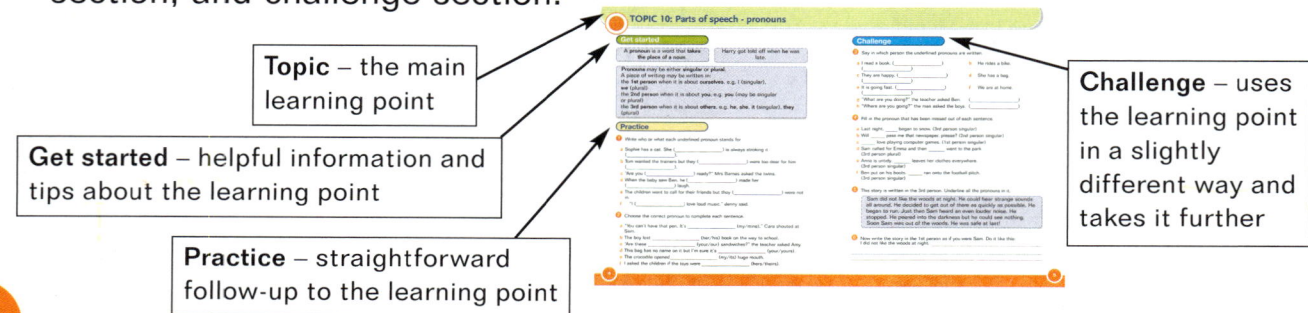

Challenge

2 **Make some rhyming words.**

a Change the **l** in **light** to **r, m, br**. Write the new words you make.

_____   _____   _____

b Change the **b** in **book** to **t, sh, cr**.

_____   _____   _____

c Change the **p** in **pound** to **f, s, gr**.

_____   _____   _____

d Change the **d** in **down** to **t, cl, fr**.

_____   _____   _____

e Change the **c** in **care** to **d, sh, squ**.

_____   _____   _____

f Change the **m** in **more** to **c, sc, sn**.

_____   _____   _____

3 **Match up the pairs of rhyming words.**
Note that the words sound alike but do not contain the same letter patterns.

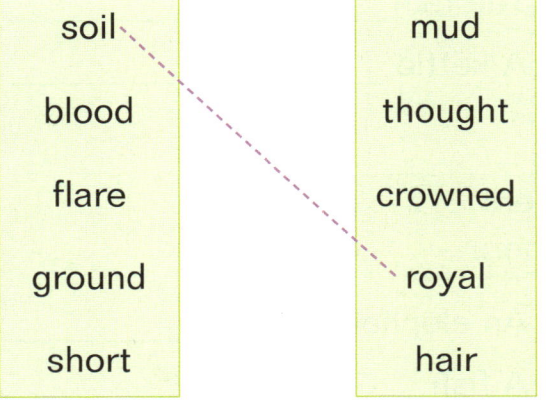

soil	mud
blood	thought
flare	crowned
ground	royal
short	hair

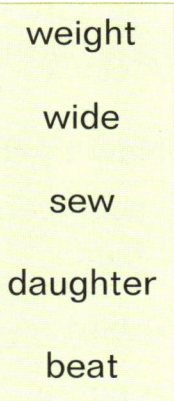

fried	weight
water	wide
hate	sew
meet	daughter
grow	beat

Topic 4: Verbs

Get started

Every **sentence** must have a **verb**.

A sentence does not make sense without one.

A verb is often a **doing** word, showing some sort of **action**.

A panda **eats** bamboo shoots.

Practice

1 Choose the correct verb to complete each sentence.

burns	ticks	hops	boils
falls	twinkles	flows	shines

a A frog _____.

b A river _____.

c A fire _____.

d A star _____.

e The sun _____.

f The rain _____.

g A clock _____.

h A kettle _____.

2 Now try these.

scampers	waddles	slithers	gallops
flies	swims	lumbers	crawls

a A bird _____.

b An elephant _____.

c A horse _____.

d A fish _____.

e A caterpillar _____.

f A duck _____.

g A mouse _____.

h A snake _____.

3 **Think of a suitable verb to fill in each gap.**

a You p_____ a picture.

b You c_____ a ladder.

c You r_____ a bike.

d You m_____ the grass.

e You c_____ a ball.

f You s_____ in a bed.

4 **Now try these.**

a You _____ a book.

b You _____ a game.

c You _____ a knot.

d You _____ your hair.

e You _____ a song.

f You _____ a hole.

5 **Choose a verb with a similar meaning to the verb in brackets in each sentence.**

baked	discovered	cleaned	bumped	jumped	mended

a I (found) _____ some money.

b I (cooked) _____ some cakes.

c I (washed) _____ the car.

d I (leapt) _____ over the wall.

e I (banged) _____ my head.

f I (fixed) _____ the broken toy.

6 **Think of a verb with a similar meaning to go in each gap.**

a I (tore) _____ my trousers.

b The car (sped) _____ round the corner.

c The boy (shouted) _____ loudly.

d The man (constructed) _____ a wall with bricks.

e The child (drew) _____ a picture.

f Sam (giggled) _____ to himself.

g The strong man (turned) _____ the iron bar.

h I (opened) _____ my present.

Topic 5: Syllables

Get started

When we say a word slowly we can hear how the word may be broken down into smaller parts, called **syllables**. Each syllable must contain at least **one vowel**.

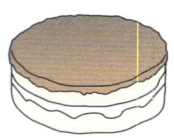

cake 1 syllable

gar/den 2 syllables

pho/to/graph 3 syllables

Practice

1 **Say each word slowly.**

Tap out the syllables as you say them.

Write down the number of syllables in each word.

a back 1	**b** about	**c** computer	**d** little
e must	**f** submarine	**g** many	**h** three
i with	**j** parachute	**k** people	**l** transporter
m would	**n** push	**o** aeroplane	**p** sister
q from	**r** strawberry	**s** because	**t** help
u brother	**v** lemonade	**w** water	**x** school
y calendar	**z** saw		

Challenge

2 Match up the first and second syllables to make some two-syllable words.

Write the words here

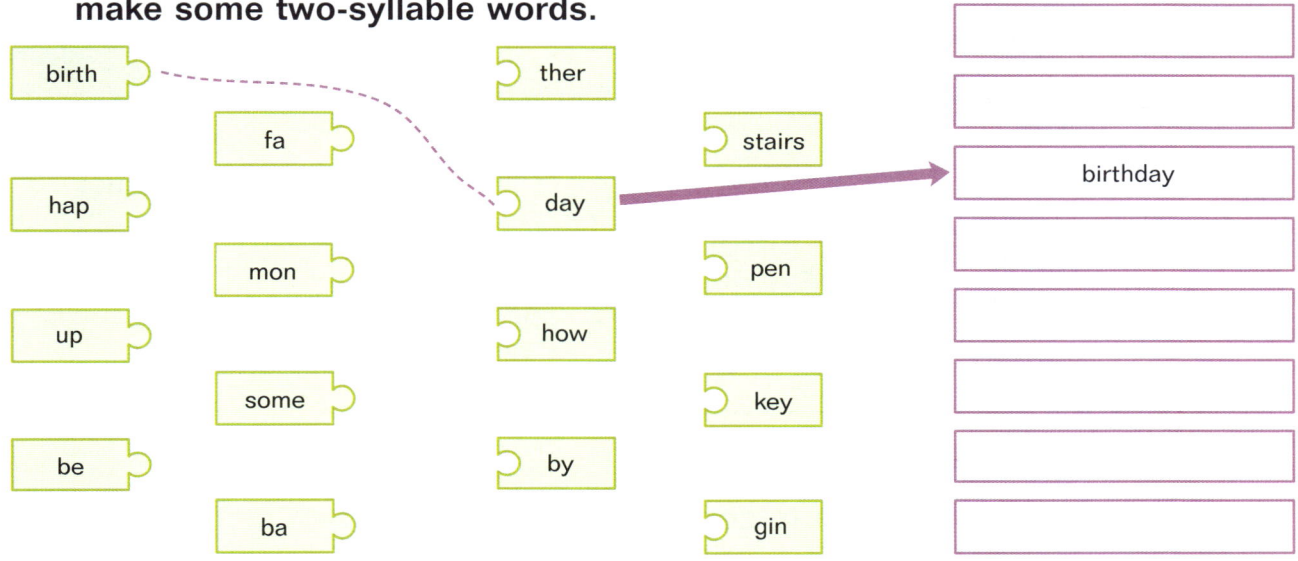

birth	ther
fa	stairs
hap	day
mon	pen
up	how
some	key
be	by
ba	gin

birthday

3 Do these syllable sums.

a al + ways = _____

b sud + den + ly = _____

c slip + per + y = _____

d let + ter = _____

e sing + ing = _____

f im + por + tant = _____

g in + side = _____

h un + der + pants = _____

i dif + fer + ent = _____

j jum + per = _____

k star + ted = _____

l re + mem + ber = _____

4 Write the words you made in the chart.

words with 2 syllables	words with 3 syllables

Topic 6: Nouns

Get started

Words that **name** things are called **nouns**.

Ordinary nouns are called **common nouns**.

A noun may be the name of a **person**, **place** or **thing**.

book
thing

teacher
person

school
place

Practice

1 **Choose the correct noun to complete each sentence.**

tap	helicopter	referee	school	vase
editor	atlas	pilot	city	burrow

a An a_____ is a book containing maps.

b A h_____ has blades that spin round to make it fly.

c Children are taught in a s_____.

d A rabbit lives in a b_____.

e A c_____ is a very large town.

f You turn on a t_____ to get water.

g A v_____ holds flowers.

h A p_____ flies an aeroplane.

i An e_____ is in charge of a newspaper.

j A r_____ is in charge of a game such as football.

Challenge

2 **Name these groups of nouns.**

a cabbage, potato, carrot   **They are all types of vegetables**.

b tennis, cricket, swimming   _____

c drums, piano, trumpet   _____

d trousers, jacket, hat   _____

e knife, fork, spoon   _____

f car, bike, coach   _____

g chair, stool, settee   _____

h shoe, boot, trainer   _____

3 **These are all names of jobs. Write what each person does.**

a vet	
b florist	
c optician	

4 **These are all names of places. Write what each place is associated with.**

a orchard	
b canal	
c factory	

5 **These are all names of things. Write what they are.**

a fence	
b envelope	
c calculator	

Test 1 (Score 1 mark for every correct answer.)

Topic 1

Choose the correct phoneme to complete each word.

1 tr_____ (ai/ay)

2 s_____t (ea/ee)

3 b_____t (ow/oa)

4 gr_____ (ew/oo)

Topic 2

Rewrite each sentence correctly.

5 the duck quacked _____

6 all cats purr _____

7 all snails have shells _____

8 a rabbit lives in a burrow _____

Topic 3

9–12 Match up each word in Set A with a word in Set B that rhymes.

Set A	mean	why	book	two

Set B	look	you	seen	high

Topic 4

Choose the correct verb from the box to complete each sentence.

| sleep | look | switch | write |

13 You _____ with a pen.

14 You _____ in a mirror.

15 You _____ in a bed.

16 You _____ on a light.

Topic 5

Say each word slowly. Write down the number of syllables in each word.

17 dinosaur ☐

18 robot ☐

19 bird ☐

20 rabbit ☐

Topic 6

Match up each set of nouns with the group name that describes it best.

21 oak   pine   ash

things you write with

22 lion   crocodile   ape

trees

23 pen   pencil   crayon

pets

24 cat   dog   gerbil

wild animals

Mark the test. Remember to fill in your score on page 3.

Write your score out of 24.   ☐

Add a bonus point if you scored 20 or more.

TOTAL SCORE FOR TEST 1   ☐

Topic 7: Dictionary work

A **dictionary** may be used to help you check the **spelling** of a word.

A **dictionary** may be used to help you find the **definition** (meaning) of a word.

Dictionaries are organised in **alphabetical order**.

apple	banana	carrot

sack	shoe	stone

These words are organised according to their **first** letter.

These words are organised according to their **second** letter.

Practice

1 Write these animals in alphabetical order according to their first **letter.**

a | bear | alligator | dog | camel |

_____ _____ _____ _____

b | panda | lion | tiger | gorilla |

_____ _____ _____ _____

c | kangaroo | goat | hippo | monkey |

_____ _____ _____ _____

2 Write these animals in alphabetical order according to their second **letter.**

a | squirrel | swan | sheep | snake |

_____ _____ _____ _____

b | hedgehog | horse | hamster | hippo |

_____ _____ _____ _____

c | crocodile | cat | cow | cheetah |

_____ _____ _____ _____

3 Each sentence contains one word which is spelt incorrectly.
Find and underline this word.

Look up the correct spelling in a dictionary.	Write the word correctly here.
a The number <u>forteen</u> comes after thirteen.	fourteen
b My favourite colour is perple.	
c You cannot write with a blunt pensil.	
d The TV programme was very intresting.	
e The hansome prince married the princess.	
f I had a biscit with my drink.	
g I went to bed at the ushual time.	
h Do you know the anser to the question?	

4 Match up each word with its correct definition. Use a dictionary to help you.

chameleon	easy to get at or use
barge	someone who looks after people's eyes
convenient	a small lizard that can change colour
flee	a sudden rush of wind
optician	a place in the desert with water and trees
juggernaut	a long canal boat
gust	a large fall of snow or rocks sliding down a mountain
oasis	where large amounts of water are stored
hangar	to run away
reservoir	a place where aeroplanes are kept
avalanche	a large lorry

Topic 8: Singular and plural

Get started

Singular means one. Plural means more than one.

We can just add s to many nouns to make them plural – but not always!

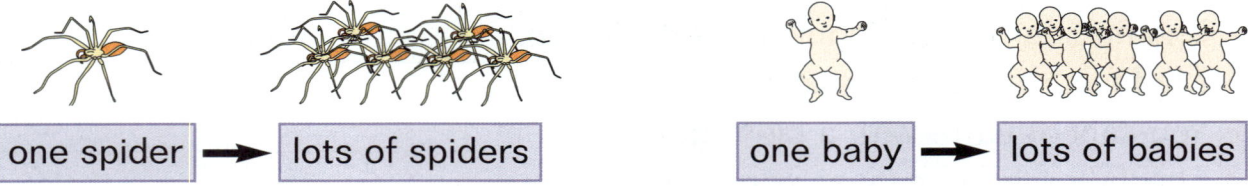

| one spider | → | lots of spiders |

| one baby | → | lots of babies |

Practice

Rule 1 If a singular noun ends with **s**, **sh**, **ch** or **x**, we add **es** to make it plural.

1 Follow the rule above and complete the chart.

singular	plural
one fox	lots of ____foxes____
one stitch	lots of _____
one wish	lots of _____
one glass	lots of _____
one arch	lots of _____
one church	lots of _____
one brush	lots of _____
one box	lots of _____
one bus	lots of _____
one bunch	lots of _____
one dish	lots of _____
one patch	lots of _____

Rule 2 If a singular noun ends with a **vowel + y**, we just add **s** to make it plural e.g. one monkey but two monkeys.

Rule 3 If a singular noun ends with a **consonant + y**, we change the **y** to **i** and add **es** e.g. one baby but lots of babies.

2 **Follow the rules above. Write the plurals of these nouns.**

one holiday	two **holidays**	one donkey	two _____
one lady	two _____	one valley	two _____
one pony	two _____	one city	two _____
one toy	two _____	one story	two _____
one lorry	two _____	one chimney	two _____
one jockey	two _____	one fly	two _____
one berry	two _____	one guy	two _____
one turkey	two _____	one body	two _____

Rule 4 If a singular noun ends with **f** (or **fe**), change the **f** to **v** and add **es** e.g. one calf but two calves.

Rule 5 If a singular noun ends with **o**, we often add **es** to make it plural e.g. one tomato but two tomatoes.

3 **Follow the rules above. Change the underlined nouns into the plural form.**
  a The <u>wolf</u> (_____) ran into the woods.
  b I picked up the <u>leaf</u> (_____) from the ground.
  c The lady put the <u>loaf</u> (_____) into her basket.
  d I peeled the <u>potato</u> (_____) ready for dinner.
  e In the distance I saw the <u>volcano</u> (_____) smoking.
  f The <u>thief</u> (_____) stole the jewels from the shop.
  g The <u>hero</u> (_____) returned from the war.
  h I put the books on the <u>shelf</u> (_____) in my bedroom.

Topic 9: Verb tenses

Get started

The **tense** of a verb tells us **when** an action took place.

I **am playing** football.

Yesterday I **played** tennis.

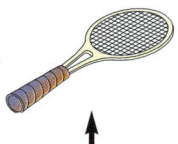

When we write about something that is happening **now**, we use the **present tense**.

When we write about something that happened **in the past**, we use the **past tense** of verbs. The past tense often ends in **ed**.

Practice

1 Fill in the correct form of the verb in each gap.

Present tense	Past tense
I am splashing in the sea.	Yesterday I ____**splashed**____ in the sea.
He is jumping on the bed.	Yesterday he _____ on the bed.
You are playing cricket.	Yesterday you _____ cricket.
She is walking up a hill.	Yesterday she _____ up a hill.
We are painting.	Yesterday we _____.
I am helping my friend.	Yesterday I _____ my friend.
You are cooking a meal.	Yesterday you _____ a meal.
He is kicking a ball.	Yesterday he _____ a ball.
She is acting in a play.	Yesterday she _____ in a play.
They are looking in a shop.	Yesterday they _____ in a shop.

Challenge

2 Write the past tense of each of these verbs. Watch your spelling!

a pop __popped__   b beg _____   c sip _____

d pat _____   e pin _____   f bob _____

3 Write the past tense of each of these verbs.

a blaze __blazed__   b scrape _____   c hike _____

d live _____   e slope _____   f use _____

4 Write the past tense of each of these verbs. Watch your spelling!

a marry __married__   b hurry _____   c try _____

d cry _____   e worry _____   f bury _____

Irregular verbs do not end in **ed** in the past tense.

5 Write each sentence as if it happened yesterday.

Today	Yesterday
I am feeling a little ill.	**Yesterday I felt a little ill.**
I am riding my bike.	
I am singing a song.	
I am eating an apple.	
I am flying to Spain.	
I am driving my car.	
I am speaking loudly.	
I am creeping about.	
I am hiding under the bed.	
I am kneeling on the floor.	

Topic 10: Proper nouns

A **proper noun** is the name of a **particular** person, place or thing.

A proper noun always **begins** with a **capital letter**.

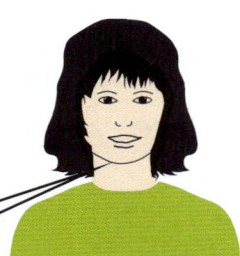

My name is **Amy**. I live in **Ashford**.

Practice

1 **Rewrite these proper nouns. Begin each with a capital letter.**

a manchester

_____

b sophie

_____

c tuesday

_____

d fir tree road

_____

e queen anne

_____

f daily mirror

_____

g paris

_____

h february

_____

i doctor khan

_____

j cardiff

_____

k liverpool

_____

l greece

_____

m river severn

_____

n red riding hood

_____

o edinburgh

_____

p buckingham palace

_____

q the regal hotel

_____

r the variety theatre

_____

s treasure island

_____

t roald dahl

_____

2 **Copy these sentences. Put in the missing capital letters.**

a mr and mrs smith went to spain on holiday.

_____

b the prime minister lives at 10 downing street.

_____

c doctor foster came to see me when I was ill.

_____

d the last day of the week is saturday.

_____

e amy and emma are good friends, but they don't like tom.

_____

f do you prefer books by phillipa pearce or shirley hughes?

_____

g the plane from athens landed at luton airport.

_____

h my favourite comic is the beano.

_____

3 **Write the name of:**

your favourite sportsperson _____

the last month of the year _____

a member of the Royal Family _____

your favourite book _____

a country beginning with B _____

a daily newspaper _____

a famous building _____

the capital city of Ireland _____

a river in Britain _____

your favourite pop singer _____

Topic 11: Adjectives

An **adjective** is a **describing** word.

It gives us more **information about a noun**.

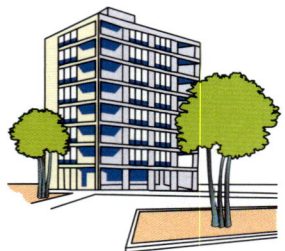

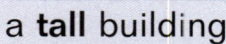

a **tall** building

a **wide** river

a **fizzy** drink

Practice

1 Underline the adjective in each of these phrases.

a a ripe banana   b a green pear   c the old house

d a windy day   e some sour lemons   f the small baby

g some buzzing bees   h a wild animal   i a beautiful actress

j some gold coins   k the rough sea   l a blunt pencil

2 Choose the most suitable adjective to describe each noun.

a a _____ pencil (heavy/sharp)

b a _____ giant (tall/rough)

c a _____ noise (loud/bold)

d a _____ mark (quiet/dirty)

e a _____ lion (fizzy/fierce)

f an _____ bottle (empty/excited)

g a _____ prince (soft/handsome)

h a _____ ruler (wobbly/straight)

i a _____ clown (fair/funny)

j a _____ meal (hot/hard)

k a _____ hill (steep/slow)

l a _____ dustbin (sweet/smelly)

3 Match up the adjectives that mean the same.

Write them here.

quick	feeble	_____
big	scared	_____
bent	horrible	_____
weak	fast	quick fast
nasty	broad	_____
frightened	large	_____
sly	dear	_____
wide	tiny	_____
expensive	crooked	_____
small	cunning	_____

4 Think of an interesting adjective to complete each phrase.

a a _____ tiger   b a _____ car

c a _____ forest   d a _____ teacher

e a _____ cave   f a _____ monster

g a_____ castle   h a _____ puddle

i a _____ drain   j a _____ nurse

5 These are all adjectives to do with feelings. Fill in the missing letters.

a s__d   b __ __y   c sc__ __ __d   d am__ __ed

e __ore__   f __ __ppy   g a__ __ry   h c__r i o__ __

i __xc__ __ed   j __ __ __ __er__ble   k __ __eas__d   l fur__ __ __ __

Topic 12: Prefixes

Get started

A **prefix** is a group of letters that goes **in front** of a word.

Adding a prefix may change the **meaning** of a word.

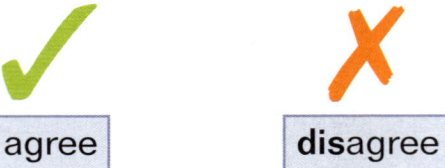

agree   **dis**agree

Practice

1 Add the prefix to make new words.

a

happy ⟶ __unhappy__

well ⟶ _____

un → fair ⟶ _____

dress ⟶ _____

lucky ⟶ _____

b

appear ⟶ _____

obey ⟶ _____

dis → agree ⟶ _____

trust ⟶ _____

honest ⟶ _____

2 Add **un** or **dis** to the beginning of each word to give it the opposite meaning.

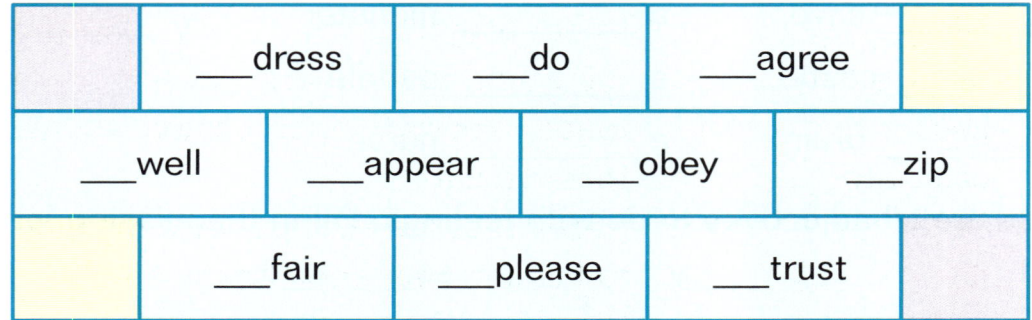

	___dress	___do	___agree	
___well	___appear	___obey	___zip	
	___fair	___please	___trust	

3 **Make these words.**

a re+turn _____**return**_____   b pre+fix _____   c pre+face _____

d re+take _____   e re+call _____   f pre+pare _____

g pre+mature _____   h re+pay _____

4 **Choose one of the words you made above to complete each sentence.**

a The baby was born too soon. It was _____.

b I could not _____ the man's name because I had forgotten it.

c The man had to _____ his driving test because he failed it.

d You add a _____ to the beginning of a word.

e I wanted to _____ home because I was tired.

f You have to _____ a loan.

g You will find a _____ at the beginning of some books.

h I wanted to _____ a meal for my mum to surprise her.

5 **Complete each word with either the prefix** mis **or** ex.
Join up each word with its meaning.

**mis** spell	to calculate wrongly
_____pand	tired out
_____judge	to make a spelling mistake
_____clude	to get bigger
_____behave	the way out of a place
_____hausted	to judge something or someone wrongly
_____calculate	to leave out
_____handle	goods that are sent out of the country
_____it	to handle a situation badly
_____ports	to behave badly
_____pronounce	to put out a fire
_____tinguish	to pronounce a word wrongly

Test 2 (Score 1 mark for every correct answer.)

Topic 7

Write each set of words in alphabetical order.

1 | tiger | sheep | rabbit | whale

_____ _____ _____ _____

2 | dog | badger | antelope | cat

_____ _____ _____ _____

3 | shake | skid | sign | seat

_____ _____ _____ _____

4 | wood | write | week | win

_____ _____ _____ _____

Topic 8

Write the plural of each noun.

5 one box but two _____

6 one baby but two _____

7 one wolf but two _____

8 one potato but two _____

Topic 9

Fill in the past tense of each verb.

present tense	past tense
9 I am helping.	I _____.
10 I am skipping.	I _____.
11 I am hurrying.	I _____.
12 I am writing.	I _____.

 ## Topic 10

Rewrite each proper noun correctly.

13 edward _____

14 spain _____

15 december _____

16 river thames _____

 ## Topic 11

Fill in the missing vowels in these adjectives.

17 h___ ___vy

18 s___ft

19 r___ ___nd

20 sw___ ___t

 ## Topic 12

Choose the correct prefix to begin each word.

21 _____appear (un/dis)

22 _____turn (re/pre)

23 _____lock (ex/un)

24 _____behave (dis/mis)

Mark the test. Remember to fill in your score on page 3.

Write your score out of 24. ☐

Add a bonus point if you scored 20 or more.

TOTAL SCORE FOR TEST 2 ☐

Get started

Where is my pen?

Stop shouting at once!

We ask a **question** to find out something. A question always **begins** with a **capital letter** and **ends** with a **question mark**.

We use **exclamations** to show we **feel strongly** about something. An exclamation always **starts** with a **capital letter** and **ends** with an **exclamation mark**.

Practice

1 **Write these questions again and punctuate them correctly.**

a how did you get wet

_____

b where is portugal

_____

c what are you doing

_____

d why are you crying

_____

e when is february

_____

f who can swim

_____

g where does milk come from

_____

h how long is it until teatime

_____

2 **Write these exclamations again and punctuate them correctly.**

a look out

_____

b it's not fair

_____

c this is terrible

_____

d what a lovely surprise

_____

e get away from me

_____

f i love strawberries

_____

g don't ever do that again

_____

h what a sensible child you are

_____

3 Copy and punctuate these sentences correctly.

Five sentences need question marks and five need exclamation marks.

a why is the dog barking

_____

b what a nice T-shirt

_____

c where is my pencil

_____

d go away at once

_____

e who is good at singing

_____

f has anyone seen my book

_____

g i hate the cold

_____

h stop shouting

_____

i what do you think you are doing

_____

j my house is on fire

_____

4 Think of someone famous.

Make up some questions you would like to ask him or her.

_____

_____

_____

_____

_____

5 Write an exclamation you might make if . . .

. . . you saw a monster _____

. . . you won the Lottery _____

. . . you fell in an icy pond _____

. . . your friend gave you a nice present _____

. . . you saw a burglar robbing your house _____

Topic 14: Subject and verb agreement

Get started

Every sentence must have a **verb**.

Every verb must have a **subject** (the person or thing that goes with the verb).

The subject and verb must always **agree**.

| The children was running. | **✗** | The children were running. | **✔** |

subject   verb   subject   verb

Practice

1 Choose was or are to fill in each gap.

a There _____ lots of apples.

b Ben _____ very tall.

c The chicken _____ clucking.

d The sun _____ bright.

e The horses _____ galloping fast.

f The leaves _____ turning brown.

g A frog _____ hopping along.

h Some ants _____ running around.

i The wind _____ blowing.

j Some birds _____ singing.

2 Choose is or are to complete each sentence.

a It _____ a lovely day.

b They _____ singing.

c He _____ asleep.

d We _____ going out.

e She _____ going home.

f You _____ not right.

g _____ it too hot?

h _____ they working hard?

i _____ you working hard?

j We _____ talking quietly.

Challenge

3 **Choose the correct form of the verb to go with each subject.**

a A duck _____. (quack/quacks)

b Most owls _____ (hunt/hunts) at night.

c The children _____ (play/plays) tennis in summer.

d Where _____ (do/does) you live?

e Some elephants _____ (has/have) big ears.

f All dogs _____ (like/likes) bones to chew.

g Tigers _____ (roar/roars) when they _____ (is/are) angry.

h My uncle _____ (snore/snores) when he _____. (sleep/sleeps)

4 **Change the subject of each sentence into the plural.**
Make the necessary changes to the verb as well.

a The pigeon was cooing.   **The pigeons were cooing.**

b The child is chattering. _____

c The girl is singing. _____

d The teacher was smiling. _____

e The cat purrs. _____

f The boy has gone. _____

g The car was going too fast. _____

h The leaf has turned brown. _____

i I am eating. _____

j It does not work. _____

Topic 15: Contractions

Contractions are words we have **shortened** by **missing out some letters**.

We use an **apostrophe** to show where letters are missing.

Please **don't** do that!

don't = do not

Practice

1 **Join up each contraction with its longer form.**

doesn't	it is
wasn't	would not
it's	does not
you're	she is
they're	was not
wouldn't	you are
she's	we have
they'll	they are
we've	I am
I'm	they will

2 **Write the contraction that means:**

a would not **wouldn't**   b they are _____   c we have _____

d I am _____   e you are _____   f she is _____

g does not _____   h was not _____   i they will _____

Challenge

3 Put in the missing apostrophe in each contraction.

Write the longer form of each contraction.

a theres   **there's**   **there is**   b youll   _____ _____

c isnt   _____ _____   d arent   _____ _____

e Ive   _____ _____   f youve   _____ _____

g wed   _____ _____   h well   _____ _____

i cant   _____ _____   j neednt   _____ _____

k itll   _____ _____   l shes   _____ _____

4 Rewrite these sentences. Replace the underlined words with contractions.

a It <u>was not</u> a very nice day.

_____

b If you try <u>you will</u> be able to do it.

_____

c I like apples because <u>they are</u> sweet.

_____

d <u>We are</u> running because <u>it is</u> late.

_____

e You <u>must not</u> shout in a library.

_____

f I <u>do not</u> want to play chess.

_____

g I <u>could not</u> open the door.

_____

h <u>I will</u> be sad if the shops are shut.

_____

i <u>That is</u> my pen on the table.

_____

j <u>I am</u> happy because <u>it is</u> Friday.

_____

Topic 16: Synonyms

Get started

Synonyms are words which have **very similar** meanings.

We can use a **thesaurus** to help us find synonyms.

a **big** sack of potatoes

a **large** sack of potatoes

POTATOES

Practice

1 **Match up the pairs of synonyms.**

Write them here.

big	start	
small	broad	big large
begin	large	
narrow	jolly	
wide	little	
happy	thin	
tired	intelligent	
clever	horrible	
hard	weary	
nasty	difficult	

Challenge

2 **Choose the most suitable synonym to replace the underlined word.**

a The princess looked <u>lovely</u> _____ in her dress. (beautiful/handsome)

b Don't <u>dump</u> _____ your rubbish in the countryside. (put/leave)

c The brave man <u>rescued</u> _____ the drowning child. (saved/helped)

d The house is <u>empty</u> _____. (full/vacant)

e I couldn't <u>stay</u> _____ any longer. (wait/lift)

f Matt had a <u>pile</u> _____ of dirty clothes in his room. (lot/assortment)

g I felt very <u>sad</u> _____. (frustrated/unhappy)

h There was a loud <u>knock</u> _____ on the door. (bang/smash)

3 **Think of a word with a similar meaning to replace the word in brackets in each sentence. Use a thesaurus to help you.**

a It was a (dark) _____ night.

b The fox was very (sly) _____.

c The flowers gave off a sweet (smell) _____.

d I got (wet) _____ in the rain.

e The man (attempted) _____ to lift the rock.

f The climber stood at the (top) _____ of the mountain.

g The flower bed is (circular) _____.

h The teacher was (sure) _____ she was right.

i The knight was very (courageous) _____.

j The doctor was a very (wealthy) _____ man.

Topic 17: Personal pronouns

Get started

A **pronoun** is a word that **takes the place of a noun**.
('**Pro**' means '**in place of**'.)

Ann got into trouble when **she** was late.

Here are the common **personal pronouns**:

| I | me | we | us | you | he | him | she | her | it | they | them |

Practice

1 **Complete each sentence. Choose the personal pronoun that makes sense.**

a The boy was thirsty so _____ (he/she) had a drink.

b _____ (I/We) am good at spelling.

c The children were excited when _____ (it/they) went on holiday.

d "What are _____ (you/she) doing?" the teacher asked Emma.

e _____ (It/I) is a hot day today.

f The girl put on her swimming costume when _____ (he/she) went in the sea.

g As the lion stood up _____ (it/they) roared.

h Have _____ (you/he) got any money?

i "Pass the ball to _____ (he, me)!" Ali shouted to Tom.

j If you annoy a wasp it will sting _____ (you, us).

k I collect marbles. _____ (I, me) keep _____ (it/them) in an old box.

l We like bees. _____ (It, They) give _____ (me/us) honey.

Challenge

2 Circle the personal pronoun on each line of this puzzle.

q	w	a	f	m	e	o	p	k	l
z	x	c	v	b	h	g	w	e	q
a	d	f	g	j	u	s	y	t	r
h	y	o	u	p	o	q	z	x	e
m	n	b	v	h	i	m	a	z	c
s	h	e	z	x	c	v	b	n	m
t	r	w	q	c	v	b	h	e	r
k	l	j	x	i	t	y	o	d	f
a	w	t	h	e	y	b	h	y	t
k	l	u	y	t	h	e	m	q	w

3 Write who or what each underlined pronoun stands for.

a I tried to read the book but <u>it</u> (_____) was too hard for me.

b My dad bought a new jumper. It looked nice on <u>him</u> (_____).

c "What a thoughtful child <u>you</u> (_____) are!" Mrs Hill said to Sam.

d "<u>I</u> (_____) love strawberries," Jordan said.

e "Come and play with <u>us</u> (_____)," Emily and Laura said.

f The babies wanted to play with the toys but <u>they</u> (_____) were broken.

g "<u>We</u> (_____) like cricket," Imran and Ali said.

h James was better at sport than Shannon, but <u>she</u> (_____) was better at art.

i William has a gerbil. <u>He</u> (_____) feeds <u>it</u> (_____) every day.

j "Will <u>you</u> (_____) make <u>me</u> (_____) a drink?" Mrs Jones asked Anna.

k Mrs Hill wanted the ring but <u>it</u> (_____) was too dear for <u>her</u> (_____).

l "Are <u>you</u> (_____) coming?" Mrs Bruce asked Robert and John.

Topic 18: Commas

I like apples, bananas, pears and peaches.

Pass me the newspaper, please.

Commas are used to **separate** things in a **list**. We do **not** need a comma **before** the word <u>and</u> in a list.

Commas are used to **separate** **extra bits** that are **added** to the **beginning** or **ending** of sentences.

Practice

1 **Copy these sentences. Put in the missing punctuation marks.**

a in the woods I saw a fox a squirrel some birds and a hedgehog

_____

b a hairdresser needs a brush a comb a mirror and some scissors

_____

c a gardener needs a spade a fork a mower and a hoe

_____

d out of the window I can see a car a lorry a bus and two bikes

_____

e for my birthday I got a ball a book a game and a watch

_____

f at the supermarket mrs brown bought some eggs a packet of cornflakes a tin of beans and a loaf of bread

_____

_____

Challenge

2 **Copy these sentences. Put in the missing punctuation marks.**

a where are you ben _____

b may i have a drink please _____

c look at my picture mum _____

d what is the matter mrs jones _____

e stop shouting william _____

f i cant do that can i _____

g yes you can _____

h ill go first shall i _____

i would you like a cake steven _____

j its my go next i think _____

3 **Complete these sentences in your own words. Don't forget the commas.**

a Four things I like to eat are _____

_____

b The first four months of the year are _____

_____

c Five things I can see out of my bedroom window are _____

_____

d In the fridge at home we keep _____

_____

e The colours of the rainbow are _____

_____

f Five big towns in Britain are _____

_____

Test 3 (Score 1 mark for every correct answer.)

Topic 13

Write these questions and exclamations correctly.

 1 where are you going
_____

2 look out
_____

3 it's horrible
_____

4 will you wait for me
_____

Topic 14

Choose the correct form of each verb to complete each sentence.

5 We _____ (was/were) laughing.

6 Sarah _____ (like/likes) apples best.

7 Cows _____ (moo/moos) a lot.

8 A tortoise _____ (move/moves) slowly.

Topic 15

Write the long form of each contraction.

9 isn't _____

10 we've _____

11 I'm _____

12 you're _____

Topic 16

Match up the pairs of synonyms.

13	brief	certain
14	sure	eager
15	huge	short
16	keen	immense

Topic 17

Write who or what each underlined pronoun stands for.

17 I wanted the bike but <u>it</u> (_____) was too dear.

18 "Can <u>you</u> (_____) come out to play?" Amy asked Emma.

19 The children tried hard but <u>they</u> (_____) did not win.

20 "<u>I</u> (_____) like swimming," Ben said.

Topic 18

Fill in the missing commas in these sentences.

21 I have a cat a dog a gerbil and some goldfish.

22 Outside my house there was a car a bus a bike and a lorry.

23 How are you Mrs Hill?

24 Be quiet Amy!

Mark the test. Remember to fill in your score on page 3.

Write your score out of 24.

Add a bonus point if you scored 20 or more.

TOTAL SCORE FOR TEST 3

Topic 19: Compound words

Get started

A **compound word** is made of two shorter words joined together.

butter	+	fly	=	butterfly

Practice

1 Do these word sums. Make some compound words.

a sun + shine = _____	**b** my + self = _____
c play + time = _____	**d** out + side = _____
e some + one = _____	**f** farm + yard = _____
g bath + room = _____	**h** grand + mother = _____
i moon + light = _____	**j** sea + side = _____
k hand + bag = _____	**l** tooth + brush = _____
m foot + ball = _____	**n** horse + shoe = _____
o butter + cup = _____	**p** lady + bird = _____

2 **Make some compound words.**

Write the words here.

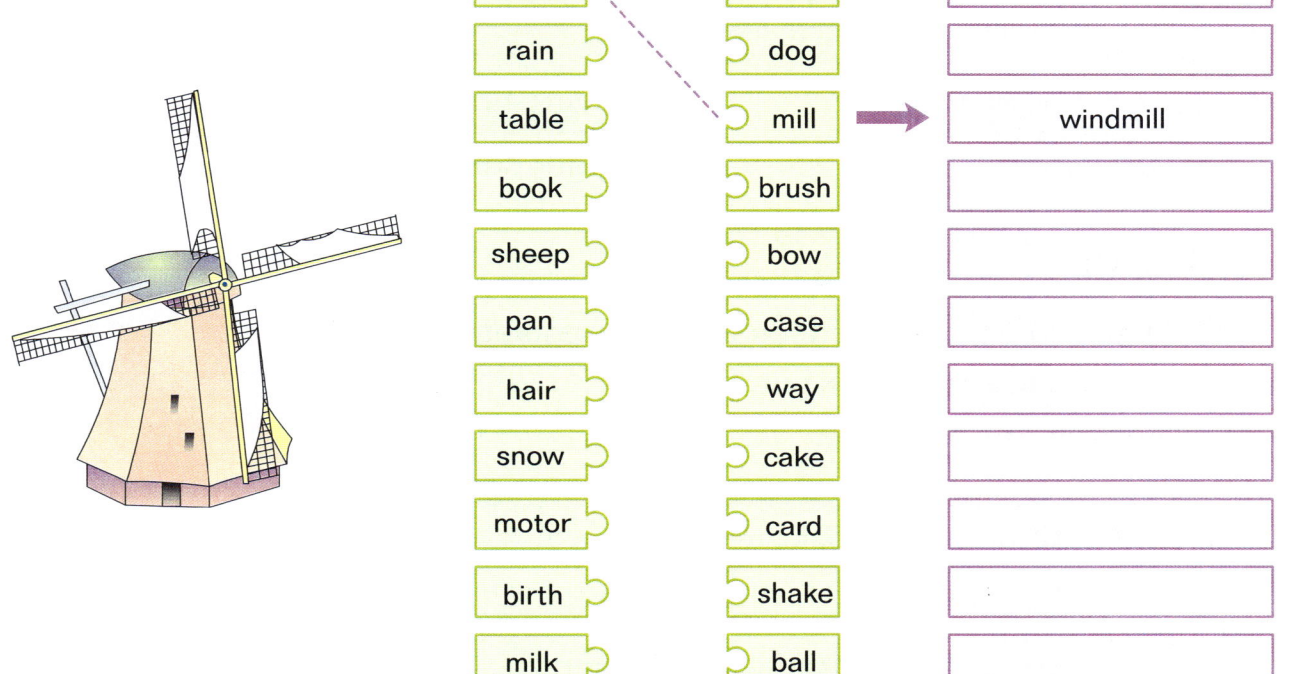

wind		cloth
rain		dog
table		mill
book		brush
sheep		bow
pan		case
hair		way
snow		cake
motor		card
birth		shake
milk		ball
post		day

windmill

3 **Join up each word in Set A with a word in Set B to make a compound word.**

| Set A | sun | book | home | water | letter | butter |
| | key | sauce | tooth | hand | motor | hedge |

| Set B | ache | hog | light | fall | hole | mark |
| | cup | way | cuff | pan | box | work |

Topic 20: Conjunctions

A **conjunction** is a **joining** word.

We use a **conjunction** to join two short sentences together to make one longer sentence.

I was tired. I went to bed.	I was tired **so** I went to bed.
two short sentences	one longer sentence with a conjunction

Practice

1 Write each pair of sentences as one long sentence.
Join them with either and **or** but.

a I sat down. I read a book.

_____

b Harry loved cabbage. William hated it.

_____

c The cat woke up. It went into the garden.

_____

d Cara has dark hair. She has brown eyes.

_____

e Cotton wool is soft. Stone is hard.

_____

f Edward got on his bike. He rode it to the park.

_____

g A hare is fast. A tortoise is slow.

_____

h Laura went upstairs. She had a bath.

_____

Challenge

2 **Write each pair of sentences as one long sentence.**
Choose the best conjunction to join each pair of sentences.

a I hurt my leg. I fell off my bike. (so/when)

_____

b Shannon got into trouble. She was late home. (because/so)

_____

c You might hurt someone. You throw stones. (if/as)

_____

d My mum was pleased. I remembered her birthday. (but/when)

_____

e It was hard to see. It was dark outside. (because/and)

_____

f My toe nails were too long. I cut them. (if/so)

_____

3 **Think of a suitable ending for each long sentence.**
Underline the conjunction in each.

a The toy had been broken since _____.

b My dog was pleased because _____.

c I was sad when _____.

d We went for a walk although _____.

e He would not have fallen over if _____.

f It was pouring with rain so _____.

g We walked through the woods as _____.

h I took a packed lunch because _____.

Topic 21: Suffixes

Get started

A **suffix** is a group of letters we add to the **end** of a word.

talk + ing = talk**ing**	wave + ing = wav**ing**	drum + ing = drumm**ing**
We can often add a suffix without **changing the spelling** of the root word.	If the root word **ends** with a **consonant + e**, we **drop the e** before adding the suffix	If the word has just **one syllable**, ends with a **consonant** and has a **short vowel sound** in the middle, we **double the consonant**, before we add the suffix.

Practice

1 Complete this chart.

root word	+ ing	+ ed
mix	mixing	mixed
walk		
paint		
box		
knock		
pour		
crawl		
cook		

2 Add y to each noun to change it into an adjective.

noun	adjective
smell	smelly
dust	
oil	
cloud	
curl	
greed	
mess	
bend	

3 **Add** ing to each verb. Spell the words you make correctly.

a write   b hide   c bake   d smile   e stare

__writing__   _____   _____   _____   _____

4 **Write** the root verb for each of the following verbs.

a argued   b gaped   c blazed   d wiped   e ruled

__argue__   _____   _____   _____   _____

5 **Add** ing and ed to each of these verbs. Spell the words you make correctly.

a hop   __hopping__   __hopped__   b wag   _____   _____

c beg   _____   _____   d hum   _____   _____

e pin   _____   _____   f tip   _____   _____

6 **Complete** this chart.

root adjective	+ suffix **er**	+ suffix **est**
wet	wetter	wettest
long		
red		
fast		
fit		
pale		
thin		
soft		
flat		
safe		
slim		
fresh		
nice		

Topic 22: Using speech marks

When we write, we use **speech marks** to show when someone is **speaking**.

We write what the person says **inside** the speech marks.

The **first letter** inside the speech marks should always be a **capital** letter.

We should never close speech marks without putting in a **punctuation mark**.

My bike is new.

Mark said, "My bike is new."

Practice

1 **Fill in the missing speech marks in this conversation.**

a Ben said, It's a lovely day.

b Sam said, It certainly is.

c Ben asked, Do you think it will rain?

d Sam replied, I don't think so.

e Ben said, I'm going for a picnic.

f Sam said, That sounds nice.

g Ben asked, Would you like to come?

h Sam exclaimed, That would be lovely!

i Ben asked, Where shall we go?

j Sam said, Let's go to the park.

Challenge

2 **Copy each sentence and punctuate it correctly.**

a sue said, look at the picture I painted

_____

b henry said, i am good at football

_____

c emma asked, do you like snooker

_____

d ali said, my uncle lives in birmingham

_____

e rosie said, may i have some new trainers

_____

f charlotte exclaimed, my mum is the best in the world

_____

3 **Fill in something each of the people might say inside the speech marks.**

a The artist said, "_____."

b The baker said, "_____."

c The dentist said, "_____."

d The farmer said, "_____."

e The hairdresser said, "_____."

f The queen said, "_____."

g The magician said, "_____."

h The pilot said, "_____."

i The sailor said, "_____."

j The referee said, "_____."

Topic 23: Possessive adjectives

Get started

Possessive adjectives tell us who something belongs to.

This is **my** bag, not **your** bag!

Here are the common **possessive adjectives**:

my	your	his	her	its	our	their

Practice

1 Find and underline the possessive adjectives in these sentences.

a I picked up my book and went to bed.

b The children emptied their bags.

c The lady lost her coat.

d The bird laid its eggs in the nest.

e "Is this your coat?" Mrs Shah asked Emma.

f "Our model is the best," the boys boasted.

g The man took off his cap.

h "I'm sure this is my book," John said.

i Anna's house has a red door so that must be her house.

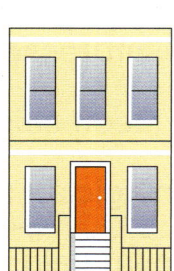

j Your picture is excellent.

2 **Choose the correct possessive adjective to complete each sentence.**

a This is _____ (my/our) toy. It belongs to me.

b The lady was sure it was _____ (her/its) coat.

c The girl lost _____ (her/its) bike.

d "No! You can't have _____ (my/our) ball!" shouted Luke and Alex.

e The man lost _____ (his/her) wallet.

f "Is this _____ (your/our) ruler?" the teacher asked Amy.

g Is this _____ (your/its) book?

h The dog wagged _____ (my/its) tail.

3 **Find the seven possessive adjectives hidden in the word-search puzzle.**
Write the adjectives here.

x	a	b	m	y	c	d	e	f	h	i	f
h	e	r	g	h	j	k	g	y	o	u	r
n	o	p	i	t	s	q	t	h	e	i	r
r	h	x	r	s	t	u	v	o	u	r	w
y	z	h	i	s	m	b	d	q	u	r	s

_____

_____

_____

_____

_____

4 **Make up some sentences of your own.**
Use each possessive adjective you found above at least once.

_____

_____

_____

_____

_____

_____

_____

_____

Topic 24: Silent letters

Get started

Some words contain **silent letters**.

We cannot hear silent letters when we say words containing them.

knot   **w**rist   **g**naw

Practice

1 Each of the words in the wall contains a silent k, w or g at the beginning.
Write the words in the correct columns in the chart.

knot	wrap	gnat	wreck	gnash
knee	wrist	knife	write	
gnome	gnaw	knock	wrong	knit
wren	gnarled	wretch	know	

silent **g**	silent **k**	silent **w**

Challenge

2 Fill in the missing silent b, l or t in each word. Use a dictionary if necessary.

a thum__**b**__	**b** fas____en	**c** ta____k	**d** crum____
e whis____le	**f** pa____m	**g** wres____le	**h** clim____
i ha____f	**j** num____	**k** this____le	**l** ca____m
m lam____	**n** sta____k	**o** cas____le	**p** com____
q glis____en	**r** yo____k	**s** ca____f	**t** fo____k
u bom____	**v** wa____k	**w** plum____er	**x** lis____en
y de____t	**z** rus____le		

3 Use the words in the box to answer each clue.

thumb	castle	bomb	plumber	numb	debt	crumb
stalk	yolk	calm	talk	palm	glisten	rustle

a The sound dry leaves make _____

b A very small piece of bread _____

c Type of tree _____

d This explodes! _____

e To shine or sparkle _____

f The opposite of angry _____

g Something you have to pay! _____

h Like a small finger _____

i You do this with your voice. _____

j Feeling no pain _____

k Part of an egg _____

l A fortified building of the past _____

m Someone who mends burst water pipes _____

n Part of a flower _____

Topic 19

1–4

Match up each word in Set A with a word in Set B to make a compound word.

Set A	wind	shoe	play	rain

Set B	lace	bow	mill	ground

Topic 20

Choose the best conjunction to fill each gap.

5 I got undressed _____ (and/but) I went to bed.

6 I like carrots _____ (and/but) I don't like cabbage.

7 I sat down _____ (if/because) I was tired.

8 My hair was too long _____ (so/because) I had it cut.

Topic 21

Add the suffix to each word. Spell the words you make correctly.

9 draw + ing = _____   **10** hope + ed = _____

11 give + ing = _____   **12** wave + ed = _____

Topic 22

Fill in the missing speech marks in each sentence.

13 Mr Barton said, I'm going out.

14 Where are you going? his wife asked.

15 I'm going to the shop, Mr Barton replied.

16 Mrs Barton said, Don't be too long!

Topic 23

Underline the possessive adjective in each sentence.

17 The boy lost his pencil.

18 Do you like my new trainers?

19 The children reached their house in time for lunch.

20 The dog pricked up its ears.

Topic 24

Each word has a silent letter missing. Write each word again, correctly.

21 nife _____   **22** nome _____

23 thum _____   **24** lisen _____

Mark the test. Now add up all your test scores and put your final score on page 3.

Write your score out of 24.

Add a bonus point if you scored 20 or more.

TOTAL SCORE FOR TEST 4

Answers

Topic 1: **Phonemes** (page 4)

1.

a. tree	**b.** pail	**c.** tray	**d.** sheet	**e.** bead	**f.** chain
g. eat	**h.** reach	**i.** deep	**j.** peep	**k.** green	**l.** seal
m. clay	**n.** rail	**o.** sway	**p.** paint	**q.** play	**r.** wait

2.

ee words	**ea** words	**ai** words	**ay** words
tree	bead	pail	tray
sheet	eat	chain	clay
deep	reach	rail	sway
peep	seal	paint	play
green		wait	

3.

a. coat	**b.** low	**c.** blow	**d.** loaf	**e.** show
f. pillow	**g.** toad	**h.** soap	**i.** elbow	**j.** shadow

4.

a. mood	**b.** new	**c.** grew	**d.** shoot	**e.** screw
f. threw	**g.** moon	**h.** root	**i.** chew	**j.** drew

5.

oa words	**ow** words	**ew** words	**oo** words
coat	low	new	mood
loaf	blow	grew	shoot
toad	show	screw	moon
soap	pillow	threw	root
	elbow	chew	
	shadow	drew	

6.
Answer will vary. Many answers are possible.

y (as in dry)	by	sty	fly
ar (as in car)	bar	mark	harbour
ir (as in shirt)	squirt	bird	whirl
ea (as in head)	dread	breath	weather
oi (as in boil)	oil	coin	point
oy (as in joy)	toy	royal	employ
ou (as in ground)	round	plough	about
ow (as in cow)	how	prowl	shower
aw (as in law)	draw	hawk	crawl
or (as in short)	cord	order	store

Topic 2: **Capital letters and full stops** (page 6)

1.

a. The pirate rowed his boat to the beach.
b. He unloaded a metal chest from his boat.
c. Inside the chest there were lots of gold coins.
d. The pirate dragged the heavy chest to a cave.
e. Inside the cave he dug a hole in the ground.
f. It made him very hot.
g. When the hole was deep enough he buried the chest.
h. Then he got into his boat and rowed away.

2.

a. The cat has five kittens. They are very fluffy.
b. The man opened the door of his car. He got in.
c. The woman came in. She was very cold.
d. The dog chased the cats. It did not catch them.

3. and **4.**
Answers will vary.

Topic 3: **Rhyming** (page 8)

1.

m<u>oo</u>n/s<u>oo</u>n, tr<u>ay</u>/sw<u>ay</u>, k<u>ite</u>/wh<u>ite</u>, c<u>one</u>/ph<u>one</u>, dr<u>ain</u>/ch<u>ain</u>, h<u>igh</u>/th<u>igh</u>, st<u>ew</u>/cr<u>ew</u>, b<u>ook</u>/h<u>ook</u>, r<u>ed</u>/b<u>ed</u>, g<u>ood</u>/w<u>ood</u>

2.

a. right/might/bright	**b.** took/shook/crook	**c.** found/sound/ground
d. town/clown/frown	**e.** dare/share/square	**f.** core/score/snore

3.

soil/royal; blood/mud; flare/hair; ground/crowned; short/thought fried/wide; water/daughter; hate/weight; meet/beat; grow/sew

Topic 4: **Verbs** (page 10)

1.

a. hops	**b.** flows	**c.** burns	**d.** twinkles
e. shines	**f.** falls	**g.** ticks	**h.** boils

2.

a. flies	**b.** lumbers	**c.** gallops	**d.** swims
e. crawls	**f.** waddles	**g.** scampers	**h.** slithers

3.

a. paint	**b.** climb	**c.** ride	**d.** mow	**e.** catch	**f.** sleep

4.
Answers may vary. For example:

a. read	**b.** play	**c.** tie	**d.** brush	**e.** sing	**f.** dig

5.

a. discovered	**b.** baked	**c.** cleaned	**d.** jumped	**e.** bumped	**f.** mended

6.
Answers may vary. For example:

a. ripped	**b.** raced	**c.** yelled	**d.** built
e. painted	**f.** laughed	**g.** twisted	**h.** unwrapped

Topic 5: **Syllables** (page 12)

1.

a. 1	**b.** 2	**c.** 3	**d.** 2
e. 1	**f.** 3	**g.** 2	**h.** 1
i. 1	**j.** 3	**k.** 2	**l.** 3
m. 1	**n.** 1	**o.** 3	**p.** 2
q. 1	**r.** 3	**s.** 2	**t.** 1
u. 2	**v.** 3	**w.** 2	**x.** 1
y. 3	**z.** 1		

2.
father; upstairs; birthday; happen; somehow; monkey; baby; begin

3.

a. always	**b.** suddenly	**c.** slippery	**d.** letter	**e.** singing	**f.** important
g. inside	**h.** underpants	**i.** different	**j.** jumper	**k.** started	**l.** remember

4.

words with two syllables	words with three syllables
always	suddenly
letter	slippery
singing	important
inside	underpants
jumper	different
started	remember

Topic 6: **Nouns** (page 14)

1.
a. atlas   **b.** helicopter   **c.** school   **d.** burrow   **e.** city
f. tap   **g.** vase   **h.** pilot   **i.** editor   **j.** referee

2.
a. They are all types of **vegetables**.   **b.** They are all types of **sport**.
c. They are all types of **musical instruments**.
d. They are all types of **clothing**.
e. They are all types of **cutlery**.   **f.** They are all types of **transport**.
g. They are all types of **furniture**.   **h.** They are all types of **footwear**.

3.
Suggested answers. (Answers may vary.)
a. A vet looks after sick or injured animals.
b. A florist sells flowers.
c. An optician looks after people's eyesight.

4.
Suggested answers. (Answers may vary.)
a. fruit trees   **b.** narrow boats   **c.** making things

5.
Suggested answers. (Answers may vary.)
a. A fence is something that makes a boundary.
b. An envelope is something to put a letter in before you post it.
c. A calculator is a machine that works out sums for you.

Test 1 (page 16)

Topic 1   **1.** tray   **2.** seat   **3.** boat   **4.** grew

Topic 2   **5.** The duck quacked.   **6.** All cats purr.
          7. All snails have shells.   **8.** A rabbit lives in a burrow.

Topic 3   **9.–12.**   mean/seen; why/high; book/look; two/you

Topic 4   **13.** write   **14.** look   **15.** sleep   **16.** switch

Topic 5   **17.** 3   **18.** 2   **19.** 1   **20.** 2

Topic 6   **21.** trees   **22.** wild animals
          23. things you write with   **24.** pets

Topic 7: **Dictionary work** (page 18)

1.
a. alligator, bear, camel, dog
b. gorilla, lion, panda, tiger
c. goat, hippo, kangaroo, monkey

2.
a. sheep, snake, squirrel, swan
b. hamster, hedgehog, hippo, horse
c. cat, cheetah, cow, crocodile

3.
a. fourteen   **b.** purple   **c.** pencil   **d.** interesting
e. handsome **f.** biscuit   **g.** usual   **h.** answer

4.
chameleon/a small lizard that can change colour;
barge/a long canal boat;
convenient/easy to get at or use;
flee/to run away;
optician/someone who looks after people's eyes;
juggernaut/a large lorry;
gust/a sudden rush of wind;
oasis/a place in the desert with water and trees;
hangar/a place where aeroplanes are kept;
reservoir/where large amounts of water are stored;
avalanche/a large fall of snow or rocks sliding down a mountain

Topic 8: **Singular and plural** (page 20)

1.
foxes; stitches; wishes; glasses; arches; churches; brushes; boxes; buses; bunches; dishes; patches

2.
holidays; ladies; ponies; toys; lorries; jockeys; berries; turkeys; donkeys; valleys; cities; stories; chimneys; flies; guys; bodies

3.
a. wolves   **b.** leaves   **c.** loaves   **d.** potatoes
e. volcanoes   **f.** thieves   **g.** heroes   **h.** shelves

Topic 9: **Verb tenses** (page 22)

1.
splashed; jumped; played; walked; painted; helped; cooked; kicked; acted; looked

2.
a. popped   **b.** begged   **c.** sipped   **d.** patted   **e.** pinned   **f.** bobbed

3.
a. blazed   **b.** scraped   **c.** hiked   **d.** lived   **e.** sloped   **f.** used

4.
a. married   **b.** hurried   **c.** tried   **d.** cried   **e.** worried   **f.** buried

5.

Yesterday
Yesterday I felt a little ill.
Yesterday I rode my bike.
Yesterday I sang a song.
Yesterday I ate an apple.
Yesterday I flew to Spain.
Yesterday I drove my car.
Yesterday I spoke loudly.
Yesterday I crept about.
Yesterday I hid under the bed.
Yesterday I knelt on the floor.

Topic 10: **Proper nouns** (page 24)

1.
a. Manchester   **b.** Sophie   **c.** Tuesday
d. Fir Tree Road   **e.** Queen Anne   **f.** Daily Mirror
g. Paris   **h.** February   **i.** Doctor Khan
j. Cardiff   **k.** Liverpool   **l.** Greece
m. River Severn   **n.** Red Riding Hood   **o.** Edinburgh
p. Buckingham Palace   **q.** The Regal Hotel   **r.** The Variety Theatre
s. Treasure Island   **t.** Roald Dahl

2.
a. Mr and Mrs Smith went to Spain on holiday.
b. The Prime Minister lives at 10 Downing Street.
c. Doctor Foster came to see me when I was ill.
d. The last day of the week is Saturday.
e. Amy and Emma are good friends, but they don't like Tom.
f. Do you prefer books by Phillipa Pearce or Shirley Hughes?
g. The plane from Athens landed at Luton Airport.
h. My favourite comic is The Beano.

3.
Personal answers.

Topic 11: **Adjectives** (page 26)

1.
a. ripe   **b.** green   **c.** old   **d.** windy   **e.** sour   **f.** small
g. buzzing   **h.** wild   **i.** beautiful   **j.** gold   **k.** rough   **l.** blunt

2.
a. sharp   **b.** tall   **c.** loud   **d.** dirty   **e.** fierce   **f.** empty
g. handsome **h.** straight   **i.** funny   **j.** hot   **k.** steep   **l.** smelly

3.
weak/feeble; frightened/scared; nasty/horrible; quick/fast; wide/broad;
big/large; expensive/dear; small/tiny; bent/crooked; sly/cunning

4.
Personal answers.

5.
a. sad   **b.** shy   **c.** scared   **d.** amazed   **e.** bored   **f.** happy
g. angry   **h.** curious   **i.** excited   **j.** miserable **k.** pleased   **l.** furious

Topic 12: **Prefixes** (page 28)

1.
a. unhappy; unwell; unfair; undress; unlucky
b. disappear; disobey; disagree; distrust; dishonest

2.

	undress	undo	disagree	
unwell	disappear	disobey	unzip	
	unfair	displease	distrust	

3.
a. return   **b.** prefix   **c.** preface   **d.** retake
e. recall   **f.** prepare   **g.** premature   **h.** repay

4.
a. premature   **b.** recall   **c.** retake   **d.** prefix
e. return   **f.** repay   **g.** preface   **h.** prepare

5.
misspell/to make a spelling mistake;
expand/to get bigger;
misjudge/to judge something or someone wrongly;
exclude/to leave out;
misbehave/to behave badly;
exhausted/tired out;
miscalculate/to calculate wrongly;
mishandle/to handle a situation badly;
exit/the way out of a place;
exports/goods that are sent out of the country;
mispronounce/to pronounce a word wrongly;
extinguish/to put out a fire

Test 2 (page 30)

Topic 7	**1.** rabbit, sheep, tiger, whale		**2.** antelope, badger, cat, dog	
	3. seat, shake, sign, skid		**4.** week, win, wood, write	
Topic 8	**5.** boxes	**6.** babies	**7.** wolves	**8.** potatoes
Topic 9	**9.** helped	**10.** skipped	**11.** hurried	**12.** wrote
Topic 10	**13.** Edward	**14.** Spain	**15.** December	**16.** River Thames
Topic 11	**17.** heavy	**18.** soft	**19.** round	**20.** sweet
Topic 12	**21.** disappear	**22.** return	**23.** unlock	**24.** misbehave

Topic 13: **Question and exclamation marks** (page 32)

1.
a. How did you get wet?   **b.** Where is Portugal?
c. What are you doing?   **d.** Why are you crying?
e. When is February?   **f.** Who can swim?
g. Where does milk come from?   **h.** How long is it until teatime?

2.
a. Look out!   **b.** It's not fair!
c. This is terrible!   **d.** What a lovely surprise!
e. Get away from me!   **f.** I love strawberries!
g. Don't ever do that again!   **h.** What a sensible child you are!

3.
a. Why is the dog barking?   **b.** What a nice T-shirt!
c. Where is my pencil?   **d.** Go away at once!
e. Who is good at singing?   **f.** Has anyone seen my book?
g. I hate the cold!   **h.** Stop shouting!
i. What do you think you are doing?   **j.** My house is on fire!

4. and 5.
Personal answers.

Topic 14: **Subject and verb agreement** (page 34)

1.
a. were   **b.** was   **c.** was   **d.** was   **e.** were
f. were   **g.** was   **h.** were   **i.** was   **j.** were

2.
a. is   **b.** are   **c.** is   **d.** are   **e.** is
f. are   **g.** Is   **h.** Are   **i.** Are   **j.** are

3.
a. quacks   **b.** hunt   **c.** play   **d.** do
e. have   **f.** like   **g.** roar/are   **h.** snores/sleeps

4.
a. The pigeons were cooing.   **b.** The children are chattering.
c. The girls are singing.   **d.** The teachers were smiling.
e. The cats purr.   **f.** The boys have gone.
g. The cars were going too fast.   **h.** The leaves have turned brown.
i. We are eating.   **j.** They do not work.

Topic 15: **Contractions** (page 36)

1.
doesn't/does not; wasn't/was not; it's/it is; you're/you are; they're/they are;
wouldn't/would not; she's/she is; they'll/they will; we've/we have; I'm/I am

2.
a. wouldn't   **b.** they're   **c.** we've
d. I'm   **e.** you're   **f.** she's
g. doesn't   **h.** wasn't   **i.** they'll

3.
a. there's/there is   **b.** you'll/you will   **c.** isn't/is not   **d.** aren't/are not
e. I've/I have   **f.** you've/you have   **g.** we'd/we would   **h.** we'll/we will
i. can't/cannot   **j.** needn't/need not   **k.** it'll/it will   **l.** she's/she is

4.
a. It wasn't a very nice day.   **b.** If you try you'll be able to do it.
c. I like apples because they're sweet.   **d.** We're running because it's late.
e. You mustn't shout in a library.   **f.** I don't want to play chess.
g. I couldn't open the door.   **h.** I'll be sad if the shops are shut.
i. That's my pen on the table.   **j.** I'm happy because it's Friday.

Topic 16: Synonyms (page 38)

1.
begin/start; wide/broad; big/large; happy/jolly; small/little; narrow/thin; clever/intelligent; nasty/horrible; tired/weary; hard/difficult

2.
a. beautiful   **b.** leave   **c.** saved   **d.** vacant
e. wait   **f.** lot   **g.** unhappy   **h.** bang

3.
Personal answers.

Topic 17: Personal pronouns (page 40)

1.
a. he   **b.** I   **c.** they   **d.** you   **e.** It   **f.** she
g. it   **h.** you   **i.** me   **j.** you   **k.** I/them   **l.** They/us

2.
me; we; us; you; him; she; her; it; they; them

3.
a. the book   **b.** my dad   **c.** Sam
d. Jordan   **e.** Emily and Laura   **f.** the toys
g. Imran and Ali   **h.** Shannon   **i.** William/the gerbil
j. Anna/Mrs Jones   **k.** the ring/Mrs Hill   **l.** Robert and John

Topic 18: Commas (page 42)

1.
a. In the woods I saw a fox, a squirrel, some birds and a hedgehog.
b. A hairdresser needs a brush, a comb, a mirror and some scissors.
c. A gardener needs a spade, a fork, a mower and a hoe.
d. Out of the window I can see a car, a lorry, a bus and two bikes.
e. For my birthday I got a ball, a book, a game and a watch.
f. At the supermarket Mrs Brown bought some eggs, a packet of cornflakes, a tin of beans and a loaf of bread.

2.
a. Where are you, Ben?   **b.** May I have a drink, please?
c. Look at my picture, Mum.   **d.** What is the matter, Mrs Jones?
e. Stop shouting, William!   **f.** I can't do that, can I?
g. Yes, you can.   **h.** I'll go first, shall I?
i. Would you like a cake, Steven?   **j.** It's my go next, I think.

3.
Personal answers.

Test 3 (page 44)

Topic 13	**1.** Where are you going?		**2.** Look out!	
	3. It's horrible!	**4.** Will you wait for me?		
Topic 14	**5.** were	**6.** likes	**7.** moo	**8.** moves
Topic 15	**9.** is not	**10.** we have	**11.** I am	**12.** you are
Topic 16	**13.** brief/ short	**14.** sure/ certain	**15.** huge/ immense	**16.** keen/eager
Topic 17	**17.** the bike	**18.** Emma	**19.** the children	**20.** Ben

Topic 18 **21.** I have a cat, a dog, a gerbil and some goldfish.
22. Outside my house there was a car, a bus, a bike and a lorry.
23. How are you, Mrs Hill?
24. Be quiet, Amy!

Topic 19: Compound words (page 46)

1.
a. sunshine
b. myself
c. playtime
d. outside
e. someone
f. farmyard
g. bathroom
h. grandmother
i. moonlight
j. seaside
k. handbag
l. toothbrush
m. football
n. horseshoe
o. buttercup
p. ladybird

2.
tablecloth; sheepdog; windmill; hairbrush; rainbow; bookcase; motorway; pancake; postcard; milkshake; snowball; birthday

3.
sunlight; bookmark; homework; waterfall; letterbox; buttercup; keyhole; saucepan; toothache; handcuff; motorway; hedgehog

Topic 20: Conjunctions (page 48)

1.
a. I sat down and I read a book.
b. Harry loved cabbage but William hated it.
c. The cat woke up and it went into the garden.
d. Cara has dark hair and she has brown eyes.
e. Cotton wool is soft but stone is hard.
f. Edward got on his bike and he rode it to the park.
g. A hare is fast but a tortoise is slow.
h. Laura went upstairs and she had a bath.

2.
a. I hurt my leg when I fell off my bike.
b. Shannon got into trouble because she was late home.
c. You might hurt someone if you throw stones.
d. My mum was pleased when I remembered her birthday.
e. It was hard to see because it was dark outside.
f. My toe nails were too long so I cut them.

3.
Personal answers. The underlined conjunctions should be:
a. since
b. because
c. when
d. although
e. if
f. so
g. as
h. because

Topic 21: **Suffixes** (page 50)

1.

root word	+ ing	+ ed
mix	mixing	mixed
walk	walking	walked
paint	painting	painted
box	boxing	boxed
knock	knocking	knocked
pour	pouring	poured
crawl	crawling	crawled
cook	cooking	cooked

2.

noun	adjective
smell	smelly
dust	dusty
oil	oily
cloud	cloudy
curl	curly
greed	greedy
mess	messy
bend	bendy

3.
a. writing **b.** hiding **c.** baking **d.** smiling **e.** staring

4.
a. argue **b.** gape **c.** blaze **d.** wipe **e.** rule

5.
a. hopping/hopped **b.** wagging/wagged **c.** begging/begged
d. humming/hummed **e.** pinning/pinned **f.** tipping/tipped

6.

root adjective	+ suffix **er**	+ suffix **est**
wet	wetter	wettest
long	longer	longest
red	redder	reddest
fast	faster	fastest
fit	fitter	fittest
pale	paler	palest
thin	thinner	thinnest
soft	softer	softest
flat	flatter	flattest
safe	safer	safest
slim	slimmer	slimmest
fresh	fresher	freshest
nice	nicer	nicest

Topic 22: **Using speech marks** (page 52)

1.
a. Ben said, "It's a lovely day."
b. Sam said, "It certainly is."
c. Ben asked, "Do you think it will rain?"
d. Sam replied, "I don't think so."
e. Ben said, "I'm going for a picnic."
f. Sam said, "That sounds nice."
g. Ben asked, "Would you like to come?"
h. Sam exclaimed, "That would be lovely!"
i. Ben asked, "Where shall we go?"
j. Sam said, "Let's go to the park."

2.
a. Sue said, "Look at the picture I painted."
b. Henry said, "I am good at football."

c. Emma asked, "Do you like snooker?"
d. Ali said, "My uncle lives in Birmingham."
e. Rosie said, "May I have some new trainers?"
f. Charlotte exclaimed, "My mum is the best in the world!"

3.
Personal answers.

Topic 23: **Possessive adjectives** (page 54)

1.
a. my **b.** their **c.** her **d.** its **e.** your
f. Our **g.** his **h.** my **i.** her **j.** Your

2.
a. my **b.** her **c.** her **d.** our
e. his **f.** your **g.** your **h.** its

3.
my, her, your, its, their, our, his

4.
Personal answers.

Topic 24: **Silent letters** (page 56)

1.

silent g	silent k	silent w
gnat	knot	wrap
gnash	knee	wreck
gnome	knife	wrist
gnaw	knock	write
gnarled	knit	wrong
	know	wren
		wretch

2.
a. thumb **b.** fasten **c.** talk **d.** crumb
e. whistle **f.** palm **g.** wrestle **h.** climb
i. half **j.** numb **k.** thistle **l.** calm
m. lamb **n.** stalk **o.** castle **p.** comb
q. glisten **r.** yolk **s.** calf **t.** folk
u. bomb **v.** walk **w.** plumber **x.** listen
y. debt **z.** rustle

3.
a. rustle **b.** crumb **c.** palm **d.** bomb **e.** glisten **f.** calm **g.** debt
h. thumb **i.** talk **j.** numb **k.** yolk **l.** castle **m.** plumber **n.** stalk

Test 4 (page 58)

Topic 19 1.–4. windmill; shoelace; playground; rainbow

Topic 20 5. and **6.** but **7.** because **8.** so

Topic 21 9. drawing **10.** hoped **11.** giving **12.** waved

Topic 22 13. Mr Barton said, "I'm going out."
14. "Where are you going?" his wife asked.
15. "I'm going to the shop," Mr Barton replied.
16. Mrs Barton said, "Don't be too long!"

Topic 23 17. his **18.** my **19.** their **20.** its

Topic 24 21. knife **22.** gnome **23.** thumb **24.** listen